WHY DO I SNEEZE?

By Madeline Tyler

©2019
The Secret Book Company
King's Lynn
Norfolk PE30 4LS

All rights reserved.
Printed in Malaysia.

A catalogue record for this book is available from the British Library.

ISBN: 978-1-78998-045-5

Written by:
Madeline Tyler

Edited by:
Holly Duhig

Designed by:
Danielle Jones

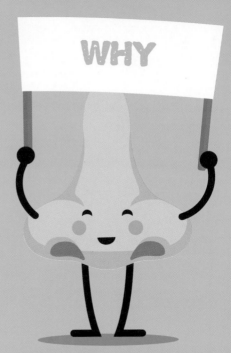
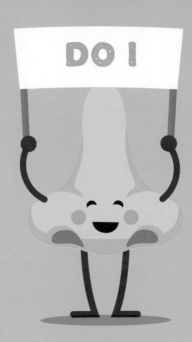

IMAGE CREDITS

All images are courtesy of Shutterstock.com, unless otherwise specified. With thanks to Getty Images, Thinkstock Photo and iStockphoto. Front Cover & 1 – LynxVector, LynxVector. Images used on every spread – Nadzin, TheFarAwayKingdom. 2 – zizi_mentos, anpannan. 4 – Niwat singsamarn. 5 – Luciano Cosmo. 6 – didiaCC. 7 – Vetreno, robuart, moj0j0. 8 – TheFarAwayKingdom, CLUSTERX. 9 – Teerapol24. 10–11 – arborelza. 12 – Top Vector Studio, BlueRingMedia. 13 – yatate. 14 – robuart. 15 – naulicreative. 16 – Korbut Ivetta. 17 – Nadia Buravleva, Wor Sang Jun. 18 – Macrovector. 19 – toranosuke. 22 – Diego Schtutman, Nadezda Barkova, ershov Oleksandr. 23 – toyotoyo, Giraphics, Roman Marvel.

CONTENTS

Words that look like **this** can be found in the glossary on page 24.

GOT SNOT?

Whether you are 6 or 106, everyone's got bogies and snot. But why?!

A-CHOO!

We breathe through our nose. Sticky bogies help to protect our bodies by catching anything harmful that we breathe in. Yucky, but useful!

TAKE A DEEP BREATH IN...

Humans need to breathe in air because our bodies need **oxygen**. Air can be very dirty and full of dust, **pollen** and germs. Our bodies do not need that stuff! Ew!

Dust and smoke make the air dirty.

Snot is like a net catching all the dirt!

Mucus – known as snot – is very important because it traps all the nasty bits from the air. This helps to keep our lungs clean.

THE RESPIRATORY SYSTEM

Nose and Mouth:

You breathe in air through your nose and mouth. They filter out any big, grotty bits such as dirt or pollen.

Mucous Membranes:

Mucous membranes are found in the mouth, nose, **trachea** and lungs. They make mucus to catch things such as dust.

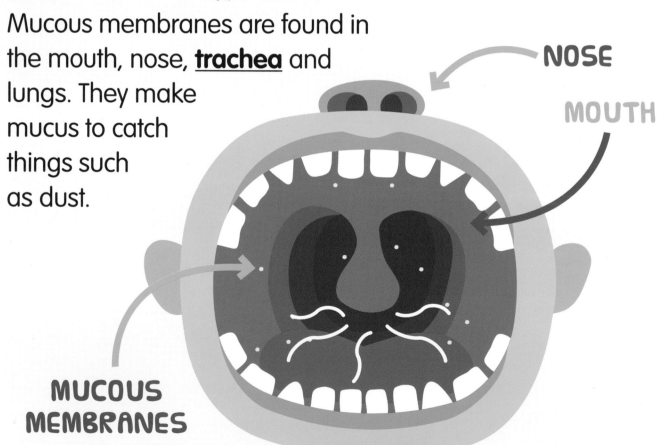

NOSE

MOUTH

MUCOUS MEMBRANES

Lungs:

Your lungs breathe in fresh air and breathe out old air.

Trachea:

Air passes through the trachea into the lungs. Sticky mucus and little hairs (**cilia**) trap anything that has gone past the nose and mouth.

TRACHEA

The trachea is joined to the lungs.

These are lungs. They help us breathe.

LUNGS

GUNGY GUARDIANS

NOSE

MOUTH

STEP 1:
Snot in your nose catches some pollen when you breathe in.

TRACHEA

LUNGS

STEP 3:
Clean air reaches the **LUNGS**, with no grotty bits in!

STEP 2:
More pollen in the air travels down the **TRACHEA**. Sticky **MUCUS** and **CILIA** stop the pollen from getting to your lungs.

11

BLOW YOUR NOSE

So, all the nasty things you breathed in are trapped in your snot. Now, how does your body get rid of it?

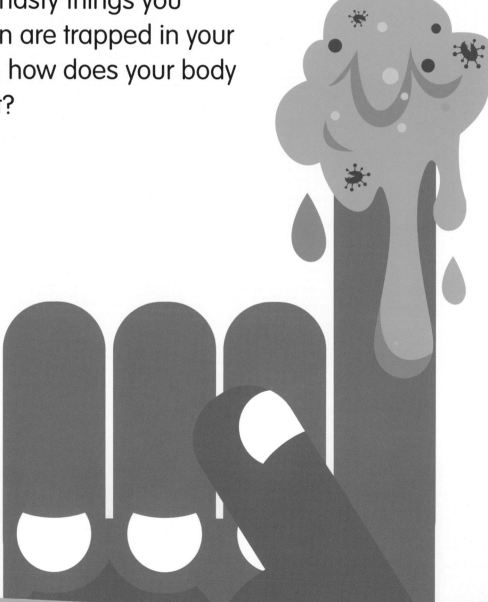

You swallow some mucus and your **stomach acid** destroys it. Other mucus dries into bogies. You can get rid of the bogies by blowing your nose.

Blow your nose into a tissue!

13

INVADERS!

Some things in the air are not just dirty, but they can also make you ill! Harmful germs can make us feel poorly.

Coughs and sneezes spread diseases!

Some germs are carried in your snot. You should always cover your nose when you cough or sneeze, so you do not make your friends ill!

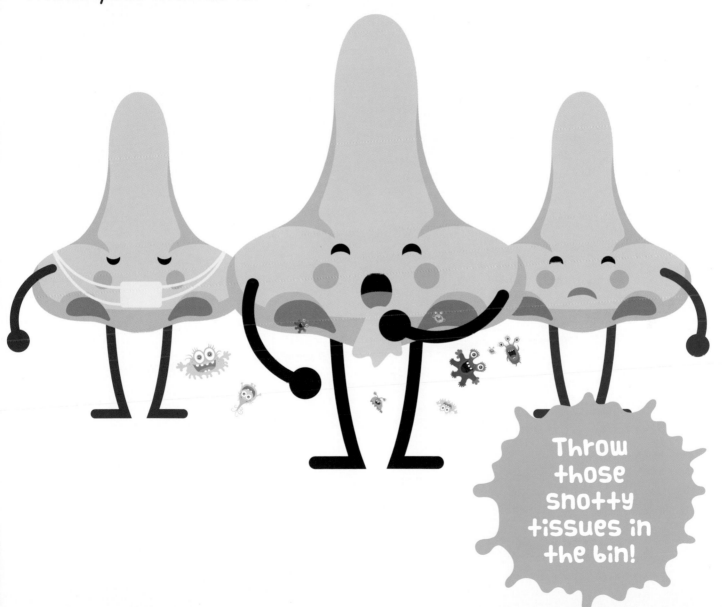

Throw those snotty tissues in the bin!

COUGHS AND SPLUTTERS

If a germ gets past the snot and into your body, you could catch a common cold. This could make you feel ill.

Colds are **contagious**! When you have a cold, it is very important to wash your hands to kill any germs.

ALLERGIES

Allergies can make people very snotty and need to sneeze a lot. Some people are allergic to cats and other people are allergic to pollen.

Cats make some people sneeze!

When a person with hay fever breathes in pollen, it irritates their nose. They produce mucus, and then sneeze to get rid of it.

WHAT SNOT HAVE YOU GOT?

What does your snot mean?

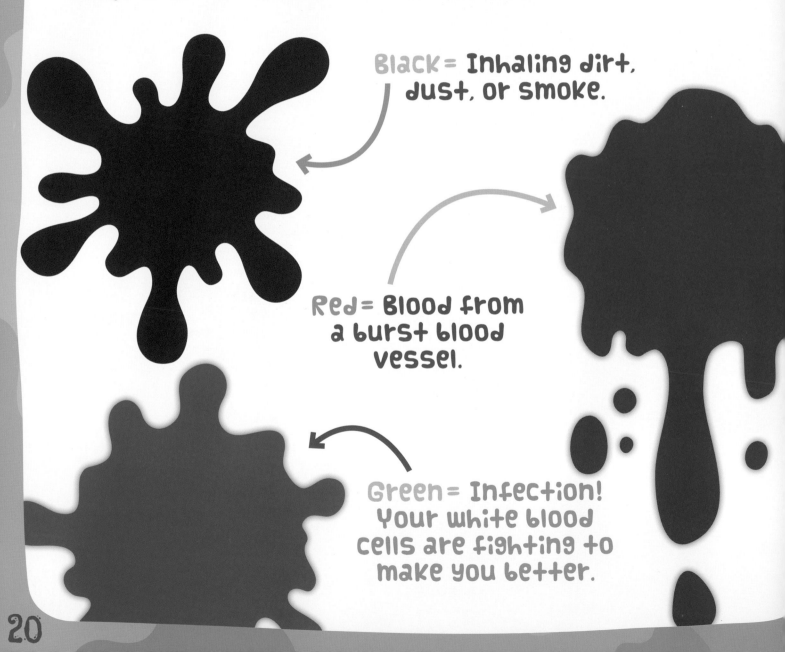

Black = Inhaling dirt, dust, or smoke.

Red = Blood from a burst blood vessel.

Green = Infection! Your white blood cells are fighting to make you better.

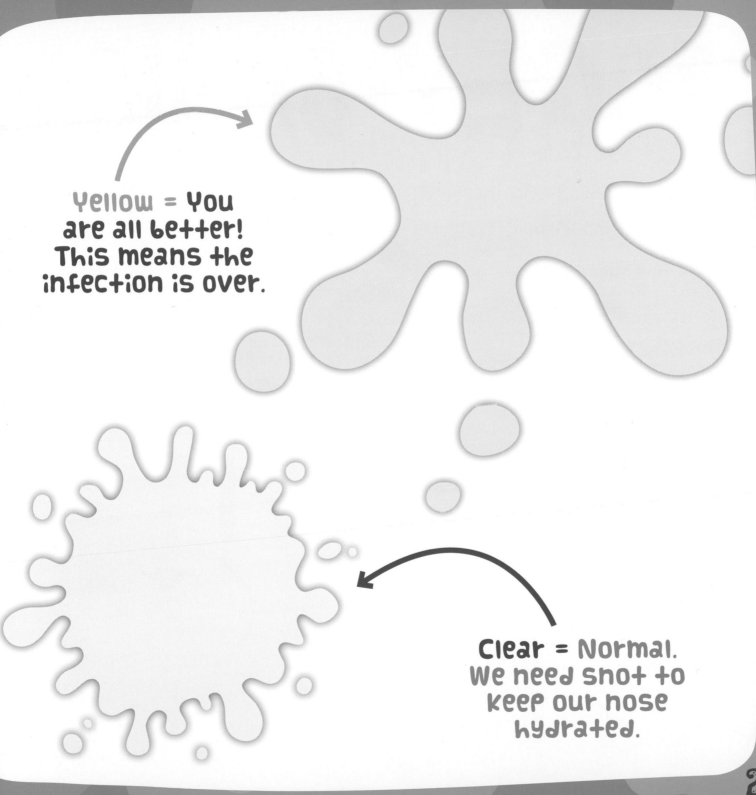

Yellow = You are all better! This means the infection is over.

Clear = Normal. We need snot to keep our nose hydrated.

BUGET BASICS

Snot droplets can fly nearly ten metres through the air!

Insects and amphibians can't sneeze!

Your nose makes a litre of mucus every day, and even more when you are ill!

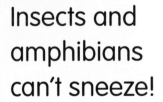

22

You cannot keep your eyes open when you sneeze – go on, try it!

Sneezes travel 50 to 96 kilometres per hour!

Donna Griffiths holds the Guinness World Record for the longest sneezing fit. She sneezed for 978 days!

GLOSSARY

allergies   when a person's body is very sensitive to something, making them sneeze or itch

cilia   little hairs found inside your body

contagious   when something such as a cold can be passed on from one person to another

mucus   slippery and sticky goo that protects your body

oxygen   something in the air that our bodies need to live

pollen   the dust found inside flowers

stomach acid   a liquid in your stomach that helps digest food

trachea   the windpipe in your throat that carries air to your lungs

INDEX